Mabel G. W. (Mabel Geraldine Woodruffe) Peacock

Tales and Rhymes in the Lindsey Folk-Speech

Mabel G. W. (Mabel Geraldine Woodruffe) Peacock

Tales and Rhymes in the Lindsey Folk-Speech

ISBN/EAN: 9783744777711

Printed in Europe, USA, Canada, Australia, Japan

Cover: Foto ©Thomas Meinert / pixelio.de

More available books at **www.hansebooks.com**

TALES AND RHYMES

IN THE

LINDSEY FOLK-SPEECH.

BY

MABEL PEACOCK.

ENTERED AT STATIONERS' HALL

GEORGE JACKSON & SON, Brigg.
GEORGE BELL & SONS,
YORK STREET, COVENT GARDEN, LONDON.
1886.

PREFACE.

YORKSHIRE and Lancashire people write in their own words about their own ways, and why should not Lincolnshire folks do so also?

Most of the books that we buy speak of strange, far-away places and persons, but this one is about things that have happened in Lincolnshire, and about every-day men and women such as we have known all our lives. Some of the stories told here are true, but the real names of the people concerned in them are not given, for perhaps they and their friends would not care to see their names in print.

As someone who does not understand the Lincolnshire dialect may chance to read

this book, it is as well to mention that in
Lindsey the letter *u* is generally pronounced
like the *oo* in foot; that the *y* in *my*,
thy, &c., is usually, though not always,
short, like the *i* in *pig*; that, as a general
rule, the vowel sounds in the pronouns are
shortened as much as possible, unless par-
ticular stress is laid on the word; that *one*,
written here *won*, rhymes with *on*; that *war*,
swarm, *want*, *wasp*, &c., have the *a* sounded
like *a* in *ant*, and that the pronoun *I* is
often sounded nearly like ā.

CONTENTS.

———◇◇◇———

TALES AND RHYMES

IN THE

LINDSEY FOLK-SPEECH.

—•◦•——

HOW IT HAPPENS THAT WE LIVE IN LINCOLNSHIRE.

—•◦•——

No one knows when men first came into England; but it must have been a long time ago, for stone knives and spear-heads have been found lying side by side with the bones of the wild beasts, that lived here before the people who knew how to use copper and iron crossed the sea and settled in this country.

In the earliest books about England we are told that the Phœnicians, who were a people near akin to the Philistines spoken

of in the Bible, used to come to Britain
(which was not called England till long
after those days) to buy tin; and the Greeks
came also to get lead, skins, slaves, and
hunting-dogs from the natives of the
country. The fore-elders of these people
had come into Britain from the stretch of
land we now call France, so the men on
both sides of the sea lived in the same way
and spoke nearly the same language.

In those days the Romans, who were
natives of Italy, had spread themselves
over all the West of Europe, and, besides
that, they had conquered the Egyptians, the
Greeks, and the Hebrews, with many other
peoples. At last they found their way to
Britain, and set to work to make themselves
masters of the country. They crossed over
the sea from France fifty-five years before
the birth of our Saviour, and, though a long
time passed by before they had conquered

the whole country, they looked on Britain
as their own from the time when they first
landed on the shore.

The Romans found the Britons lived by
cultivating the land, by cattle-breeding, and
by hunting. They dressed themselves in
checked cloaks and in skins, and they lived
in huts built of wood, or made of the reeds
that grew in the bogs. When they went
out to fight they drove in war-chariots with
scythes fixed to the axles, and they defended
their towns by digging deep ditches round
them, and by setting up walls made of trees,
felled in the neighbouring forests.

These Britons were very fond of fighting,
but they were no match for the Romans,
so they had to give way before them, and
own themselves beaten. Then the Romans
began to make roads, to build towns, and
to drain the low land by the rivers. In
Lincolnshire they built a beautiful city,

which they called Lindum Colonia, and which we now call Lincoln. They had another town at Horncastle, and another at Caistor, which place gets its name from the Roman word *castra*, a camp. At one time the shire must have been full of houses built by the Romans, or by the Britons, who tried to copy Roman ways. Bits of their broken bricks, drain-tiles, and pottery may be dug up near most of the villages in Lincolnshire.

The road running from Wintringham to Lincoln, and from Lincoln right down into the south of England, Tilbridge Lane, and the Foss-way, were all Roman roads. They made the Foss-dyke also, and used it for carrying off the water from the low land near Lincoln, and for bringing boats full of corn up to the town.

No doubt the Romans were hard masters to the people they had conquered, but they

taught them how to build good houses, and
they improved trade in all ways. During
the time that they ruled the country the
Britons learnt to work the land so well that
they were able to sell a great deal of corn
and other farm-stuff to foreigners. It was
while the Romans were here, too, that missionaries first came into the country, and
taught both the Romans and the Britons to
give up the old heathen religions and believe in Christianity. Nearly all the people
were converted, and many churches were
built; but before very long such misfortunes
came upon the whole land that all religion
seemed to be lost. For, after a while, the
Roman government in Italy and in the conquered countries began to grow weak, and
the Roman soldiers had to leave Britain
and go home to help their own people.
Then the Scotch tribes, who had been
kept in order by the soldiers, came down

from the North into South Britain and
began to spread themselves over the land,
murdering the people, burning the villages,
and driving off all the cattle they could
lay hands on.

In, or about, the year 450—that is, more
than fourteen hundred years ago—the poor
Britons did not know which way to turn
for help.   They had enough to do fighting with the people who came out of
Scotland,   but   at   this   time   a   greater
trouble fell on them.   The men of the
countries we now call North Germany,
Holland, and Denmark, began to cross the
sea, land on the British shore, and carry
off all the women, children, and cattle
they could find; thus the Britons had to
struggle against two sets of enemies at
once.   At last it struck them that it
would be a goo¹ plan to get the sea-

robbers from Germany and Denmark to help them against the Scots; so they invited them to take a share in their battles, which invitation these Angles gladly accepted, for they liked nothing better than knocking other people on the head. When, however, the Scots had been driven away, and the Britons wanted these soldiers to go back to their homes again, they would not hear of any such thing, but said they meant to stay where they were. What was worse, they sent over the sea for their friends and relations, and told them to come over and settle in the land which the Britons were too weak to defend. It was in this way that the Angles, or English, first came into the country, and changed its common name from Britain to England. These English were all heathens, and believed in many gods.

They thought that the greatest of the gods was named Woden, or Odin, that he was very wise, and that he knew all the things that were going to happen on the earth. Thor, Thunnar, or Donner, was the god of thunder and fighting; and when there was a heavy thunderstorm, the people used to think that the god made the lightning by throwing his heavy hammer at the wicked devils who were always going about bewitching men and cattle. The days of the week are still called after the old heathen gods and their mates. When we say Wednesday, we mean the day of Woden. Thursday is Thor's day, and Tuesday, Friday, and Saturday are named after gods. As the English were very fond of fighting, they had learnt to be skilful in making shields, spears, bows, arrows, swords, and battle-axes, besides which they used heavy clubs set over with iron spikes. With these weapons they drove the Britons quite away from the eastern side of the country, till they had chased them into Cumberland, Wales, and Cornwall; then they settled down in the empty towns and villages, and took the land for themselves. A great many English came into Lincolnshire, and gave their names to the villages which are still to be found there. Those places whose names end in *ham* and *ton* are nearly all called after English settlers. Messingham was, no doubt, the village of the Messing tribe. Elkington got its name from the people called Elking, and Donnington from men named Donning. A tribe or a family used to settle down together, and hold a stretch of land as common property, though each man had a separate house. The plough-

B

land and the hay-fields generally lay near
the houses in the middle of the township,
and outside was the grazing-land, where
the cows and horses ran in the summer.
Besides these closes and open fields, there
were many acres of boggy land, where the
people could catch fish and wild ducks,
and there were also forests from which
they fetched wood for building their
houses and for burning in their fires.
Many kinds of wild beasts lived in the
uncultivated land in those days: wolves,
deer, and wild cattle were to be found all
over England. The herds of pigs which
the English kept ran in the forests, too,
and fattened on the acorns of the great
oaks which grew there. As time went
on the people began to find that they
could work the land better if each man
had a share to himself, so they divided

the plough-land and meadow into lots.
But still the land did not always stay
in one man's hands during the whole of
his life; for in many places the people
met together and dealt it out again,
after a certain length of time had passed
away. All the people who had a right
to the land were freemen, and could vote
at the public meetings of the villages,
or of the set of villages that formed
a hundred; so they had the power of
choosing the men who acted as magis-
trates or filled other public offices.

Besides these freemen there were people
who held land on condition that they
worked for the landowner, or gave him a
share of what they got from the land.
These men were not free, for they could not
leave the village to settle in another township; they had not a right to vote, and in

B 2

many cases they could not marry till they had paid a fine to the master of the land on which they lived. But all the same they were not slaves. The landowner had to help them if they were too weak to guard themselves against any enemy that might try to get the better of them, and he could not make them leave their farms so long as they paid him the fixed rent of the land.

The real slaves were men and women who had been guilty of crimes, or the children of such men and women; for, unfortunately, the children of slaves were slaves, too, no matter whether the poor things had done any wrong or not. In some cases poor people who could not get bread to eat sold themselves and their little ones into slavery; but this only happened when times were very bad.

In the year 597—that is, about thirteen

hundred years ago—the people of Kent were converted to Christianity by a missionary, sent from Rome by Saint Gregory the Great, who was Pope at that time. It is said that one day, when Saint Gregory was walking in the market-place at Rome, he saw some fair-skinned, flaxen-haired lads standing there ; so he asked who they were, and the slave merchants who owned them told him that they were Angles or Englishmen, and that they had been sold by their parents. Then Saint Gregory said, " These beautiful boys ought to be called Angels, not Angles," and he made up his mind to go to England and preach the faith of Christ to the people there. But the men of Rome said they could not spare him, for he was one of the best and cleverest priests in the world ; so, as he was not allowed to do the work himself, he sent Augustine, a monk, with forty other missionaries, to preach the Gospel in England. After the conversion of the people of Kent, and of the rest of the south of England, many missionaries came further north, and one of the followers of St. Chad, the priest who converted the people of mid-England, came into Lindsey, and taught the men, women, and children to give up their heathen ways and believe in Christ. This missionary was called Higbald, and from him the church and village of Hibbaldstowe take their name. Other good men went into the north of England to convert everyone who would listen to the Gospel. Nearly a hundred years went by before all the English became Christians, because many of the heathens liked their old religion so much that they did not want to give it up. It was not easy for fighting-men to learn to forgive their enemies and to do good to those who hated them, for it seemed to them much more sensible to take a club and knock a man's brains out if he did not behave properly. Still, they did not mind much when their wives and children were converted; so little by little the missionary got all the people to leave their old beliefs and try to live like Christians.

After a time rich men began to build churches and religious houses, in which priests and monks lived, and kept schools, for the sake of the boys and young men who wanted to learn more than their fathers and mothers could teach them. Crowland Abbey, in the south of Lincolnshire, was one of these religious houses. Pious women, too, lived in companies together, and taught the girls and young women, and before long England was full of religious and learned

people. This was a very happy time for
the country, for both the rich and the poor
people left off many of their rough and
cruel ways, and began to think more of
living in peace and quiet than of fighting.
But in the year 832 great misery fell on
the land, for fresh tribes of sea-robbers
began to sail up the rivers and burn the
villages, just as the English had done when
they came to settle in Britain. These new-
comers were heathens who knew nothing of
Christ; so, after killing all the men they
could find, they stole the gold and silver
ornaments out of the churches, seized the
women and children, and destroyed every-
thing that they could not carry away in
their boats. Year by year, when the east
wind blew in spring, these pirates would
come sailing over the sea to land on the
English shore, and year by year English

men and women sent up the prayer, " From the fury of the Northmen, deliver us, O Lord," while their enemies marched through the country slaying all who tried to stand against them. Sometimes the robbers built a winter camp in a place where the English could not attack them; but no matter whether they went back to their own homes, or stayed here during the cold weather, they were always ready for their cruel work when the summer came round again, and set on the English with their long swords and heavy battle-axes, giving them no rest till they had taken the best land in the east and in the north of England for their own families to live on. Lincolnshire was full of Northmen, and we may still find out where they made their homes by counting the names of the villages that end in *by* and *thorpe*, for these two words in their language meant dwelling-place and village; so Aslackby is the dwelling-place of a man named Aslack, and Thoresthorpe means the village of Thor. Algarkirk in South Lincolnshire was most likely named after a man named Algar, who built a church at that place after the Northmen were converted to Christianity. For when the English found they could not drive their unwelcome visitors away, they set to work and taught them to give up their belief in Odin and Thor and become good Christians. Lincoln and Stamford were both celebrated towns in the time of the Northmen. Grimsby was also a well-known place, and is mentioned several times in the poems written by the Northmen. Gainsborough, too, was visited by the men of Denmark, Sweden, and Norway, and we know from old books that Swegen, King of Denmark, sailed up the

Humber and Trent, and after spending some time in Lincolnshire, died at that town in 1014. Cnut, his son, who was a wise man and brave soldier, made himself king of England, and ruled very justly, treating the English as fairly as he did his own people, the Danes. This king was not born a Christian, but he became one. It is said that one day when his servants and friends were trying to flatter him by saying that he was so powerful that even the sea would obey him, he ordered his throne to be placed on the sea-shore, and then, sitting on it, with his crown on his head and his kingly sceptre in his hand, he said to the rising tide, "Come no further," pretending to believe that the water would do as he told it. Of course the sea went on creeping up the sand, till at last it wetted his feet, and then he turned to his servants and said to them :

"The power of kings is but vanity. He only is king who can say to the ocean, '*Thus far shall thou go and no further.*'"

Unfortunately, Cnut's children were not so wise as their father. Two of his sons followed him in turn on the English throne; but they were bad and foolish men, who thought more of feasting and drinking than of their duty to the country over which they ruled. After the death of these two Danes, Edward, a man of the old English royal family, was put on the throne; but the Northmen still kept the land they had won in Lincolnshire and in other counties, and they did not lose it all even when William, the Duke of Normandy, came over from France and made himself king. This duke, and many of the people who followed him, were of the same blood as the Northmen. Their forefathers had made themselves masters of a part of France; and, as they were named Normans, that is, Northmen, the land they took was called Normandy after them. Duke William claimed the kingship of England because Edward had left him the throne by will; but the Englishmen did not want to have him in the country, so they tried to drive him over the sea again. Harald, the prince who led the English army, had just won a great victory over a band of Northmen and Englishmen who had turned against their own country, when he heard of the landing of the Norman Duke. Without taking time to rest he marched down from Yorkshire into the south of England, and met the enemy at a place in Sussex now called Battle, from the great fight which was fought there between the English and the Normans. After a bloody struggle, Harald was killed by an arrow, the English fled, and Duke William remained master of the field. Soon he was master of England too; for though the people tried to rise against him and drive him away, he and his fighting-men were far stronger than they were, so in the end they had to give way. Hereward of Brunn, who took his name from Bourn, in Lincolnshire, was a celebrated Englishman who held out for a long time against the Duke; but at last he had to submit to William, who became king of England, and was called William the First, or William the Conqueror.

This William came into England in the year 1066—that is, rather more than eight hundred years ago—and since his days the country has never been conquered by a foreign nation. The Normans spoke French for many years after they settled here, but they could not hinder the English speaking their own language. After a while, they themselves began to speak English too, and when that happened, all the people in the land became one nation. The Britons in Wales kept to their own tongue; but the Normans, Danes, Englishmen, and most of the Britons who lived in England, learnt to use one language and live under one kind of law.

By this time the old ways of managing the land had changed a good deal in Lincolnshire and in the other English counties. The king was supposed to own all the land, and he gave it out in lots to his friends on condition that they would fight for him when he needed help. Then his friends divided it out again into smaller lots among the men who promised to help them if they had any fighting to do; and these people dealt it out again on the same condition, or on condition that the tenants would work for them so many days a week, or give them part of the stock and crop at the end of the year. Sometimes the rich men were cruel to the small land-holders, but generally they got on very well together, for, though some of the farmers were bondmen and could not leave the township when they wished, their masters could not take the land away from them while they went on paying the rent agreed on.

When William the Conqueror came to England there were no slaves in Lincolnshire, so we may very well believe that the Northmen had done away with the custom of holding slaves. It is known that the priests, monks, and other pious people were very kind to poor folks, and that they often freed children who had been sold, so, perhaps, they helped the Northmen in this work.

The priests did a great deal of good in another way. While the king, and the fierce barons who held land under him, taught men the use of the sword, spear, and battle-axe, and trained them to guard the country, the priests, monks, and nuns spoke of lead-ing holy and quiet lives, and showed people how to cultivate the land, rear cattle, and do house-work in the best way. A few years after the Norman conquest, a bishop began building the great Cathedral at Lin-coln. This church was accidentally burnt down; but a new one was soon raised on its ruins, and some years later another bishop enlarged the Cathedral, by building the choir, the eastern transept, and the chapter-house, making it one of the most beautiful churches in the world.

c

About seventy years after William the Conqueror came to England, a great quarrel took place between two of his grand-children. Stephen, one of his grandsons, said that he ought to be king, because no woman had a right to reign in England; but his cousin Matilda, who was the daughter of the king who had just died, declared that she had a right to be queen, as there was no law against a woman ruling the English people. This quarrel led to a long war, and many battles were fought before the question was settled. The city of Lincoln was twice besieged by Stephen, who, how-ever, only succeeded in taking it once; for before he could get it into his hands a second time he was made prisoner by Matilda's friends. The quarrel was at last ended by an agreement which gave Stephen the throne during his life, with the understanding that Matilda's son Henry should be king after him.

This son of Matilda was crowned in London when he became king, and afterwards he was crowned again at Lincoln, which was then one of the most important towns in England. In the reign of Henry's son, John, a war broke out because the king wished to take all liberties from his subjects. The barons, the Archbishop of Canterbury (who at that time was Stephen Langton, a Lincolnshire man), the bishops, and many of the yeomen rose against the tyrant, and declared that no freeman should be imprisoned, made an outlaw, or have his land taken away from him, unless he were lawfully declared guilty of crime by a court of his peers—that is, of his equals. The barons were to be tried by barons, and the simple freemen by freemen. When the

king would not consent to this, they fought
against him till he was obliged to grant
what they asked for. Then they drew up
the list of laws called *Magna Carta*, or the
Great Charter, and made the king put his
seal to it. These laws are looked on as
the foundation of the liberties of England,
though of course changes have been made
in them since they were first written.
Though King John was forced to sign this
charter, he never meant to obey it ; and as
soon as he had the power to do so, he began
to ill-treat his people again ; so the barons
offered the kingship of England to a
French prince, who gathered an army and
came over the sea to fight against John.
John was soon hunted down into Norfolk,
where he took shelter among the people of
Lynn. Then, finding he must go north-
ward, he crossed the Wash and reached

Swineshead Abbey, in Lincolnshire, though he nearly lost his life in so doing, for before he had got safely off the sands of the Wash the tide came rushing in, and swept away a great part of the company that was crossing with him. He himself reached the shore ; but many of his companions were drowned, and his crown and other kingly ornaments were swallowed up by the sea. When he had reached Swineshead, King John fell ill, and not long after leaving that place he died. Most likely his sickness was a low fever, caught in the fens of Lincolnshire ; but many people thought that the king had been poisoned by a man who heard him say, while they were sitting together at supper in Swineshead Abbey, that he would make a half-penny loaf cost a shilling before the year was out.

After the death of John, the barons,

who had called the French king's son over
the sea, thought they could do without him,
and told him that he might go home again.
This, however, he did not wish to do; so his
army fought against the English at Lincoln, and the English won the day.   Then
the Frenchmen were obliged to leave the
country, and John's son was set on the
throne.   In the years that followed Lincolnshire was not much troubled with wars,
though a great deal of fighting went on in
different parts of England.

In the year 1366, a grandson of the
king then reigning was born at Bolingbroke
in Lincolnshire.   This child, who, from his
birthplace, was named Henry of Bolingbroke, grew up to be a very clever man, and
after the death of his grandfather, he drove
his cousin off the throne and made himself
king in his place.   This act caused a great

war in England in after-days, for a constant
quarrel about the heirship to the throne
went on. So many bloody battles were
fought, and so many people were beheaded
or hanged, that nearly all the royal family
and many of the nobles were killed off
before the dispute was settled. In the year
1485 a great battle was fought in Leicestershire, and the prince who won it made himself king, and put an end to the war by
marrying the heiress of the family who
fought against him. After this the country
was more quiet; but in the next reign new
trouble came on England. The king at
that time was Henry the Eighth. At
first he governed his people very well, but
after many years of married life he took
it into his head that he wanted to divorce
his wife, because she had only one living
child, a daughter, and he wished for a

son. So he wrote to the Pope and asked
him to say that the queen had never been
a lawful wife, and that the king might
marry again. But this the Pope refused
to do, saying he would have no hand in
such wickedness. Then King Henry had
to think of another way of getting rid of
his wife, and the plan he thought of was
this. He declared that it was a great
mistake to think that the Pope was head
of the Christian Church on earth ; and that
he himself was head of the Church in England, and, having said this, he divorced the
queen and began to take away the land
given for religious and pious uses. Some of
the rich people were glad to help the king
in this work, because he gave them a share
in the land which he seized; but many
well-to-do people and nearly all the work-
ing men and women were very angry

when they saw the property taken by the greedy king. The bishops, abbots, and clergy had generally been kind and charitable, and had helped poor folks who could not earn enough to live upon; but the friends of the king thought only of their own advantage, and did nothing for their needy neighbours. Now, when the men of Lincolnshire got to understand what had happened they came together under the leadership of the Abbot of Barlings, saying that the new law the king had made was a wicked one and ought not to be obeyed; but as they were not trained to fighting Henry's soldiers soon drove the poor fellows back to their homes again. Some of them were taken prisoners and executed at Tyburn, near London, with the Abbot of Barlings and the vicar of Louth, who had led them. After this defeat the people of

Lincolnshire had to submit to the laws of the king, but still they only gave him outward obedience. When Henry sent his men about the country to arrest the priests who held the old religion and said the king was not the head of the Church, the people used to hide them away in their houses and barns, or in the woods near the villages. This wicked king had many Catholics hanged or burnt because they would not change their religion, and he was just as cruel to the Protestants who thought it right to follow the teaching of the Bible instead of doing what he told them. Nearly all his subjects, no matter what their religion was, were glad when the brute fell ill and died. This king was not more than fifty-six years of age at his death, but in his not very long lifetime he married six wives, two of whom he had beheaded, two others he divorced, while one died a natural death, and the last one was fortunate enough to outlive him, though once, when he was angry with her, she ran a very narrow risk of having her head taken off.

In the reign of Henry's son both Catholics and Protestants were persecuted if they would not pretend to believe in the established religion. This king, who died when he was sixteen, was followed on the throne by his sister Mary, who had been brought up a Catholic before her father quarrelled with the Pope, and who had always believed in the old religion. She is often called "bloody Mary" because many Protestants were put to death during her reign, though her government was no more cruel than that of her brother, or of the sister who was queen after her, for they persecuted all Protestants and Catholics who did not believe what the Government taught them. In those days nearly all good people thought that men and women who held views different from their own about religious questions were very wicked and ought to be put to death, for fear they should teach their wrong way of thinking to other persons.

It was in the reign of Mary's sister, Elizabeth, that the first poor-law was made. Before the Church lands had been taken away poor people had had little difficulty in getting help when they were out of work, but after this loss the working-men and their families had a great deal to suffer. To make matters worse the money of most of the *Guilds*—which were societies something like the Odd-Fellows' and Foresters' Clubs—had been seized by the Government during the reign of Henry's son, so the poor people lost their friends, the rich clergy,

and their own savings also, and had nothing
left to fall back on when they could not get
employment. At that time, too, there
was a great deal of misery throughout the
country, because men who held large estates
found it pay better to lay their land down
to grass than to plough it, so many people
who had lived by cultivating the soil were
thrown out of work. Besides this trouble
there was another very serious one. The
small landowners in many villages had, as
years went by, either sold or lost the right
of feeding their cattle on the common lands,
fetching wood from the forest, and fishing
in the rivers and becks ; so the little farmers
were nearly as badly off as the day-labourers,
and it was no wonder that a poor-law was
needed to help people who were quite unable
to help themselves. In Queen Elizabeth's
reign the first English colony was founded

in America.   America had been discovered during the reign of her grandfather by an Italian sailor named Christopher Columbus, who had persuaded the king of Spain to lend him men and ships to go across the sea which washes the west coast of Europe, saying that he was sure there must be land on the other side of the water.   Before Columbus found America, potatoes, turkeys, Indian-corn, tobacco, and many other useful things, were quite unknown here; so we owe a great deal to the sailor who crossed the wide sea in search of the land which is still called the "New World."   In later years the greater part of North America was taken by the English, who drove the natives away, or killed them off, and then settled down on the newly-gained land, just as their forefathers had done in England hundreds of years before.

Queen Elizabeth never married; so at her death her cousin James, the king of Scotland, was made king of England also, and since his time both countries have had the same kings or queens. James was followed on the throne by his son Charles the First, who got into sad trouble because he wished to raise taxes without the leave of Parliament. The English people saw very well that, if the king were allowed to tax the country without first getting the consent of the men who were chosen by the voters to sit in parliament, the whole nation would soon be ruined, so they refused to let the king take their money. The king raised his war-banner at Nottingham in 1642, and soon after he did this, a battle was fought between the men who took his side in the quarrel and those who thought that the Parliament and its followers were in the right. Neither party gained much advantage that day ; but, after a struggle for power which lasted some years, the Parliamentary soldiers conquered Charles's men, managed to get the king himself into their own hands, and then tried him and put him to death.

In the early part of the war, Gainsborough, which was looked on as an important town, because it stood on the Trent, and could easily be supplied with food and arms, was held for Charles by the Earl of Kingston ; then the place was taken for the Parliament by Lord Willoughby of Parham, who, however, did not manage to keep the prize long, for the Marquis of Newcastle came and seized it again for the king. In the year 1644 Oliver Cromwell and his soldiers appeared before the town, took it again for the Parliament, and, putting men into the place to hold it against Charles's forces, marched off for York.

In 1643 a skirmish had taken place near Horncastle. This battle was called Horncastle or Winceby fight, and a lane in the neighbourhood is still called "Slash Lane" in memory of the king's soldiers who were killed there. In the year 1658 a party of the Cavaliers, as the people who fought for Charles were called, came out of Yorkshire into Lincolnshire and marched to Lincoln, where they opened the prison and let out all the prisoners. Then they went to the bishop's palace, which Captain Bee, a woolen-draper, and thirty other men defended against them for three hours. At the end of that time the Cavaliers set fire to part of the house, and by this means made the men inside yield the place to them. Then they took Captain Bee

D

prisoner, and carried him and all his wares and goods, with the money and arms they found in the palace, away to Gainsborough. When the news of this reached Rossiter, the Parliamentary Colonel who held Belvoir Castle in Leicestershire, he gathered all the troops that could be spared from the neighbouring counties, and marched into Lincolnshire; and, learning that Sir Henry Cholmondeley and his soldiers were near Gainsborough, and would hinder the Cavaliers from ferrying over the Trent and so escaping, he made for that town. When he had got about half way, he met a Captain Taylor, who was in command of a troop of horse from Lynn. They agreed together to camp for the night in Waddingham fields, near Lincoln; then, the next day, they marched through Lincoln towards Gainsborough. But, as Colonel Rossiter learnt from a man who had been taken prisoner by the Cavaliers and had got away from them, that the enemy had drawn off from Gainsborough and marched towards Newark, he altered his course and followed the king's men to Willoughby, a place about seven miles from Nottingham. Here he and his troops, with the help of some gentlemen and freeholders of Lincolnshire and Leicestershire, and the further aid of seventy or eighty men from Derbyshire and Rutland, defeated the Cavaliers and took many of them prisoners. Though this was not a great battle, it must have been looked upon as a fine victory by the Lincolnshire people, most of whom took the Parliamentary side in the war.

In King Charles the First's reign, several Dutch engineers came into England to drain the fens and bogs. Some of them got leave to settle in the Isle of Axholme in North Lincolnshire, and many a quarrel rose between them and the men of the Isle, who thought that the Dutchmen would drown the good land while they were trying to get the water off the bad.

The draining of the fens in the south of Lincolnshire was also begun about this time. But the war between the king and Parliament, as well as the ill-will of the Fen-men, prevented the work going on quickly, so many years went by before it was finished.

After King Charles had been beheaded, Oliver Cromwell, the great Parliamentary soldier, took on himself the government of the country. Though he had only the title of Protector, he was far more powerful than most kings, and ruled in the way he thought best, instead of asking what the people and

Parliament wished to do. As he was backed up by the army which had conquered Charles he could do just as he liked, and there is no denying that he was a tyrant, though on the whole he was a wise and good one, who did well by his country. When he died his son was Protector for a few months, but he soon gave the work up, so the eldest son of the late king was put on the throne. This man and his brother, who reigned after him, both wished to govern in opposition to the will of the Parliament; so some of the great English families banded together, drove the family away, and put Mary, the eldest daughter of the king, and her husband, the Prince of Orange, on the throne. After Mary and her husband were both dead, the next daughter, Anne, was made queen, and at her death the kingship was given to a German prince, who was the nearest Protestant heir to the Crown. The king who had been driven away was a Catholic, and a law had been passed that no Catholic should reign over England and Scotland.

George the First, the German prince, was the great-great-great-grandfather of the present Queen. Soon after he came to England, the old royal family tried to get back the throne again, and they tried once more during the reign of his son; but they did not succeed in the undertakings, for, though many men wished to bring them back again, a great many more were glad to be rid of them, as they did not want a set of kings who could not understand that the people of a country ought to have a share in the government.

In the year 1745, when the last attempt

to restore the outcast royal family was made, those Lincolnshire people who were on King George's side were afraid that the enemy would pass through Lincolnshire on the way to London from Scotland; so they began packing up their most valuable things and getting ready to run away, if there should be any need to do so. Fortunately for them, the Scotch soldiers never came near Lincolnshire, though several of King George's troops passed through Stamford on their way to the North. On April the 16th, 1746, the king's son, William Duke of Cumberland, defeated Charles Edward Stuart, the heir of the old royal family, at Culloden, in Scotland. This was the last battle fought in the island of Great Britain.

It was during the reign of George the Second that John Wesley, the founder of Methodism, began to preach. He was born at Epworth, in the Isle of Axholme, which town was also the birth-place of Kilham, another, but less known, religious teacher, who was the founder of the New Connexion Methodists.

In the reign of George the Third, the present Queen's grandfather, many of the open fields which lay round Lincolnshire villages were enclosed. Till that time, wide stretches of land had been left uncultivated; but as the population grew greater it was found needful to take in the wild grazing land and cut it up into closes in which corn might be grown. Some of the open commons which lay near the Trent were warped, so that a stretch of country which had hardly grown anything for the use of man was turned into very good corn and potato land. When the enclosures were made most of the small freeholders sold their common-rights, or exchanged them for a piece of the land newly taken in; but in a few villages, commons and common-rights still remain, and in these places the old English way of managing the land is partly kept up. A man who has a cow-gate in the public pasture owns that cow-gate, because hundreds of years ago, when the English came over the sea and dealt out the land, it was the custom to keep the grazing ground in common, and let every landowner run a certain number of cattle on it.

In the year 1764 England began to get into difficulties with her American colonies, for the king, and some of the men who governed under him, wished to make the colonists pay taxes, whether the Colonial Parliaments consented or not; just as Charles the First had wished to make Englishmen pay a hundred years before.

The Americans, who knew well enough
how their forefathers had withstood the
king who tried to oppress them, said flatly
that they had not settled in a new country
with the intention of being robbed of their
rights as freemen, and declared they would
only pay the taxes that their own repre-
sentatives thought just and reasonable.
Then, when the king and the English
Government tried to get the better of them,
they broke into open rebellion, and said
that they would not let the King of
England, or any other king, be their
master.   On the 4th of July, 1776, thirteen
united colonies declared themselves to be
free and independent States, and set up a
government of their own.   But though the
United States and England are now separate
nations, they have the same language and
the same blood, for many Englishmen have

gone, and still go, to settle in America ; so we speak the exact truth when we call the Americans our cousins. Many Lincolnshire people have relations in the United States and in the other countries which have been taken by Englishmen, and now the descendants of the Britons, Romans, English, Northmen, and Normans may be found in all parts of the world, carrying English ways and English words to lands which their fore-elders never heard of.

TH' LAD 'AT WENT OOT TO LOOK FER FOOLS.

WONCE when I was sittin' i' frunt o' th' Pywipe, doon by river at Lincoln, a man cum'd up wi' wou o' them theare barges an' sets hissen doon, an' efter a bit we gets to talkin', an' hed a pot o' beer together. He was fra oot 'n Oxfordsheer, an' he tell'd me a rum taale aboot foaks 'at liv'd i' them parts, an' said it was all on it as trew as Bible; bud I'm o'must fit to think 'at he'd putten a bit or two to it hissen, to top it up like. Well, he tell'd me 'at ther' was an' owd man an' his wife, an' thaay'd gotten a nice bit o' land o' the'r awn, an' a nice bit o' munny i' bank an' all. An' thaay'd

nobbud won bairn, a doughter; an' wench
hed a sweetheart 'at was call'd Jack. An'
won daay owd man was i' gardin' a diggin'
taaties, an' he thinks to hissen, " If I hev'n't
liv'd here five an' tho'ty year, an' niver
putten noä paales roond well! Why, if
oor Polly marries Jack, an' hes a bairn, it's
saafe to get i'to watter an' droond itsen!"
Then he sits doon an' falls to cryin' an'
groänin', an' oot cums his wife an' axes him
what aails him. " Why," says he, "if oor
Polly weds Jack, an' hes a bairn, it's tied
to fall doon yon well an' get droonded."
" Ey, that's sarten," says owd woman, an'
doon she sits an' begins sobbin' an' gooin'
on fit to kill hersen. Then oot cums lass
an' all, an' axes, " Whativer's matter noo ?
Hes Jack happen'd owt ? " " Naay," says
owd man, "nobbud well isn't fenced off,
thoo knaws; an' if thoo and Jack gets

married and hes a bairn, it's saafe to fall i'to watter an' droond itsen." "I niver thowt o' that afoor," says lass, "bud it's ower trew," an' she was soon agaate o' cryin' an' all. An' theare thaay stan's beälin' an' carryin' on, till thaay'd o'must wept enif to fill a wesh-tub brimful o' watter. Well, it happens 'at Jack cums up laane an' fin's 'em belderin' all of a raw. An' he axes 'em if coo's tekken wrong waay, an's deed i' cauvin'. "Naay," says owd man, "it isn't that." "Bank hesn't brokken wi' yer munny, hes it?" says Jack. "Noä," says owd woman, "it's not that." "Well then," says Jack, "what's up wi' yĕ all?" An' thaay tells him 'at it's a oppen well, wi'oot a cage roond it, an' 'at if he weds Polly, an' Polly hes a bairn, it's saafe to fall i'to watter an' get droonded. Well, when he heerd 'at thaay

was makkin' all this to-do aboot a nowt
o' that soort, he gets as mad as a beär,
an' says, "I'll tent it fra droondin', I
weant niver get married at all, if supposin'
I can't fïn' three foäks as is as blaam'd big
fools as you, afoor I've gotten a pair o'
new boots worn oot." Then he claps
gardin' gaate to wi' a bang, goäs to shop
an' buys hissen a pair o' new boots, cuts
hissen a esh-plant, to notch doon all
fools he fïn's on, an' starts off to look fer
softest foäks he can leet on i' all cuntry-
side. Well, afoor long he cums to a stack-
yard, an' seäs a man rare an' throng
shuvelin' summats up ageän stacks wi' a
scowp, nobbud ther' wasn't nowt at all
i' scowp, an' soä Jack axes him what he
reckons he's doin' on. An' man says "I'm
shuvelin' sunshine up to dry corn as was
led when it was ower weet, bud I doän't

seäm to get noä fo'ther wi' it." "Well, if
iver I seed a born fool, thoo's him," says
Jack. "Why doänt t' set sheäves up i'
stooks i' sun? Thaay'd dry fast enif then."
"I niver thowt o' that afoor," says man;
"bud awiver, I'll try it noo," an' he flings
doon shuvel, fetches his stee, an' begins to
teär stack top off. An' Jack cuts a mark
o' his stick, an' goäs a peäce fo'ther. An'
afoor he'd gotten far he cums up o' a man
'at's tryin' to reäst a cobble-stoane oppen
wi' his knife. "What art tĕ doin' on?"
axes Jack. "Why," says man, "I want
to get ken'il oot'n this here stoän, bud
knife's that blunt it slips an' slithers
i' stead o' gooin' in." "Here's anuther on
'em," thinks Jack, an' notches his esh-
plant ageän, an' then he says to man,
"Thoo mun get a hammer an' breäk
cobble, if tĕ wants to knaw what's i'side

on it." "By goes!" says man, "that thowt niver cum'd i'to my heäd, bud I'll seä what I can do noo." Well, Jack goäs a bit fo'ther, an' afoor long he cums to an' owd thakt barn 'at's grawn ower wi' gress, an' he seäs a man sittin' upo' rig, a tryin' to lug a coo up a-top on barn by a band roond it neck. An' he axes man what he's a doin' on. An' man says, "There's a rare lot o' gress up here, an' I haate to seä it waasted; nobbud I can't get coo up to eät it—she's that stewpid, the moor I pull won waay the moor she pulls t'uther." "This caps all," thinks Jack, an' he cuts anuther nick i' his stick, an' says, "Get yer hook, soft un, an' cut gress of 'n thack, an' fling it doon to coo, then she'll eät it fast enif." "Lau'sy'me," says man, "if I'd nobbud heerd tell o' that waay afoor, I shouldn't ha' choäk'd such 'n a many coos wi' this here

E

band;" an' he teks off to look fer his hook.
Bud Jack begins to think 'at Polly an' her
feyther an' muther isn't noä softer then
gen'rality o' foäks, an' soä he goäs back an's
married afoor he's gotten a munth's weär
oot'n his new boots. An' owd man put a
raalin' roond well; nobbud when childer
begun to cum ower thick an' fast he pulls it
up ageän, an' says to his wife, 'at he's sewer,
if Loord meäns to tek 'em, a bit o' fencin'
wean't stan' i' his roäd. Bud not long efter
that theäse here burial-clubs cum'd up, yĕ
knaw, an' then bairns begun deein' afoor
iver thaay was big enif to creäp doon
gardin' to well. If Loord didn't tek 'em,
sum'ats else did, soä thaay niver hed
chanche to fall i'to watter an' droond
the'rsens—an' that's th'end o' taale.

TH' MAN AN' TH' BOGGARD.

THER' isn't noä boggards here-aboots 'at I
knaw on, bud when I liv'd i' No'thampton-
sheer I heerd tell o' won 'at reckon'd 'at
best farm i' loordship belonged to him, if
ivrywon hed the'r awn, an' he let foäks
knaw it an' all. One daay he cums to man
'at hed bowt land a peäce back, an' says 'at
he mun quit. Well, at fo'st man taks noä
noätice on him whativer, an' maks as if he
didn't seä him, nor hear him nayther; bud
at last, when he begins to get fair stall'd on
his witterin' an' knaggin', he says 'at boggard mun tek law on him if he wants to get
houd o' land. He wean't gie it up till he's
maade. Then boggard chaanges his tune,

E 2

an' says, "I tell yĕ what it is. Me an' you
'll goä shares. I'll tek hairf stuff off 'n
land, an' you'll tek t'uther hairf. We wean't
hev' nowt to do wi' them lawyers. I haate
'em wo'ser then I haate gingey-beer 'ats hed
kerk left oot." Well, man says 'at he does
n't want to mak hissen i' noä waays awk-
'ard, soä he'll let boggard goä shares.
"Nobbud, we mun sattle won thing fo'st
off," says he, "an' when we've sattled it
we mun stick to it. Will yĕ tek what
graws aboon grund, or what graws beneän
grund?" Then boggard studies a peäce,
an' efter a bit he says, "I'll tek what graws
aboon grund, an' I'll cum an' fetch it at
back-end, when you've gotten ivrything in."
Then man thinks to hissen, "If I'm to hev'
all 'at's beneän grund, I'll set taaties Boggard mun tek taatie-tops an' welcome."
Soä when sattlin'-time cums, an' boggard

wants to hev' his share o' crop, man's as
ready as owt, an' lets him hev' all twitch
an' such-like kelter 'at's cum'd up, as well as
taatie-haums. But boggard doesn't feïl
clear suited, an' soä he says, " We'll swap.
I mun hev' all 'at graws beneïn grund next
time." "All raight," says man; " nobbud,
yĕ knaw, you mun stick to it noo you've
said it." Then he saws wheät, an' when
boggard cums i' fall, man gets corn an'
straw, an' boggard gets nowt bud stubble.
Well, at fo'st off he was real foul aboot it,
an' says as lawyers can't be no-how wo'ser
then this here; but efter a bit he cools
doon, an' then he tells man 'at next time
thaay moan't share crop oot, thaay mun start
mawin' it together, an' eäch on 'em mun
tak what he maws. Man didn't think a
deäl to this here waay o' goin' on, fer boggard look'd as strong as a six-year-owd

hoss, an' his airms was o'must as long as
teäkle-powls ; bud, awiver, he says to hissen
'at he'll manage to get o' his blĭnd side yit.
An' soä him an' boggard sattles at it's to be
i' that how, an' then boggard goäs awaay as
pleäsed as a dog wi' two taails. Bud when
harvest-time's cum'd roond, man goäs to
blacksmith's shop, an' gets blacksmith to
maak him a lot o' iron rods 'at's aboot as
thick as a claay pipe shank. Then he goäs
an' sticks 'em up amung corn at boggard
falls to maw, fer he'd sawn wheät agaän
that year an' all. An' he waaits till boggard cums wi' his greät long scythe, an'
thaay starts fair an' sets to wark. Bud
afoor long boggard's scythe cums agen won
o' th' iron rods, an he says, " My wo'd, bud
theäse here docks is straange an' hard to
cut." Then scythe edge catches agen
anuther on 'em, an' he stops to whet, an'

co'sses an' sweärs all time; bud ivry swing o' scythe maade things wo's, an' at last he says, " I'm that hot yĕ mud wring my shet oot, let's knock off an' hev' a bit o' bacca." " Bacca! " says man, "what can yĕ be thinkin' on? Why, yĕ hev'n't mawn a rood yit. I sha'n't gie ower till eleven, an' it's nobbud just goin' eäght by owd che'ch clock." Well, when boggard hears this, he flings doon his scythe an' says, " Yĕ maay tek mucky owd land, an' all 'at's on it. I wean't ha' nowt moor to do wi' it. I'm as sick as a toäd on it, an' on you an' all." An' off he goäs an' niver cums back noä moor. Bud foäks says 'at man took scythe hoäm wi' him, an' 'at it's hingin' i' his barn noo, to testify to trewth on it.

THE LASS 'AT SEED HER AWN GRAAVE DUG.

———◦———

Did I niver tell yĕ aboot oor Bessie, gran'-
muther, 'at seed her awn graave dug, poor
lass? It's a queer taale that, an' ivry wo'd
on it's trew. She was a real pretty lass,
wi' flaxen hair an' blew ees, an' ther' was a
man, call'd Fox, 'at was straange an' fond
on her. Well, he maade a deïl on her, an'
when he'd gotten his awn wark dun, he'd
tidy hissen up a bit, an' then he'd walk
ower to her feyther's hoose, an' help her to
milk coos, sarve pigs, an' such-like. Foäks
reckon'd he was clear soft aboot lass, bud
gell's feyther, 'at haated to seä him loongin'
aboot plaace, alus said, " He's ower keän by

hairf, an' yĕ knaw, 'When luve's ower strong it niver lasts long.'" Awiver, noä-body bud th' owd wimmin took noä noätice on him. Ivrybody knaw'd 'at he thowt 'at lass could ha' gotten her wark dun wi'oot ony o' Fox's help, an' gotten thrif it a deäl sharper an' all, an' soä foäks nobbud laughed when he carried on. Well, won daay when her feyther was oot a singlin' to'nups, Fox cums an' says, " I've gotten to goä to markit to-morrer. If tĕ can, cum to th' big esh i' Galley-daales, an' then I can seä yer hoäm, an' we'll sattle aboot gettin' married." "That's a long waay to walk," says lass, " an' it's a straange loänly roäd, an' I should be fine an' scarr'd if I met owt." Bud at last Fox gets her talk'd ower an' she says she'll be under th' esh a bit efter seven, an' then off he goäs. Well, that neet th' lass hed a straange queer dreäm, an' she says to hersen next daay, " I hedn't that theare dreäm fer nowt. I'll be i' Galley-daales afoor he tell'd me, I reckon ; then I shall get to knaw what he's up to." Soä she gets her wark dun, an' then she shuts off to Galley-daales wi'oot saayin' nowt to noäbody. An' when she gets to big esh-tree, she climbs up, an' hides hersen i' th' beughs, an' sits as still as a beä. An' efter a bit Fox cums, an' pulls a spaade oot'n hedge-bottom, an' begins to dig a graave aneän th' esh. He was that throng wi' it, he niver looked up an' seed th' lass. An' efter he'd gotten it dun, he walks up an' doon, smookin' an' lookin' at graave, an' talkin' to hissen. Well, he waaited, an' waaited fer lass till he was stall'd, bud she niver cum'd, an' at last he shuvels mouds i'to graave agaän, an' goäs awaay, chunterin'. Then lass slips doon, an' runs hoäim, as quick as if a boggard was efter her. An' next daay, when Fox cums an' axes why she'd bauk'd him i' that how, she says, " I'll tell th' if tĕ can mak this here oot :

> Riddle me, riddle me righ,·
> Up i' th' beughs so high ;
> Th' wind it blew,
> Th' cocks thaay crew,
> Th' leäves did shaake,
> My heart did aache
> To seä th' hoäle
> Th' fox did maake ;
> Riddle me, riddle me righ."

An' when Fox hears this he was fer makkin' off; bud in cums lass's feyther, wi' five or six uther men, an' teks him strīght awaay to prison. An' if it hedn't been fer that theare dreäim, 'at was sent her, lass wo'd ha' been mo'der'd, as trew as I stan' here.

T' CURATE 'AT CAAME FRA LUNNUN.

It's straange an' eäsy to laugh at parsons, an' I've dun it mysen times enew; bud I gev' it up fer good a peäce back, an' I'll tell yĕ fer why. Mr. Beulah cums to me, an' says, " I've gotten a curate cummin' fra Lunnun, an' I want yĕ to tek him in. That parlour an' best chaamber o' yours is just th' plaace to suit him, an' he's that quiet he wean't be noä waays i' yer roäd. He'll alus be set a reädin' his books an' things, when he isn't at che'ch, or runnin' aboot efter poor foäks i' parish." Well, my wife gets rooms ready, puts up cleän white winder-cot'ns, sets chiney dogs an' praayin' Samuel up o' mantil-shelf, spreäds my gran'muther

patchwork quilt upo' bed, an' meks ivrything as cumfortable as cumfortable, an'
curate cums afoor weäk-end. Well, he'd
nobbud been wi' us a neet or two, when I
says to my wife, "Mr. Beulah hed raight on
it when he tell'd me 'at curate was a quiet
un. Why, he sticks to his books as if he
was glew'd to 'em." "Ey," says she, "if
he'd a bit less larnin', an' a bit moor sense,
it wo'dn't be noä ho't to him. What's th'
good o' his books an' things when he
hardlin's knaws if cauves is born wi' horns
upo' the'r heäds or no? Them foäks i'
Lunnun mun ha' straange queer waays o'
bringin' bairns up. I niver seed such 'n a
knaw-nowt i' all my born daays." Well,
we tried to insense him aboot things, bud it
wasn't noä good. You mud as well ha'
talk'd to a stoän, as talk'd to him. He was
that scarr'd o' hosses an' beäs', an' things,

'at we hedn't noä peäce wi' him. Why,
won Setterda', when I was awaay at Don-
caster, an' my wife an' th' lass was throng
i' th' hoose, cleänin' up fer Sunda', th' owd
poll-coo kep' him fra hairf-past-three to five
i' a corner o' th' hoam-cloäse, an' he niver
hed sense to remember 'at she was blïnd
o' one ee, an' he mud ha' gi'en her slip
an gotten i' to the o'tchard wi'oot her
knawin' owt aboot it. I beleäve he'd ha'
been stood theäre yit if oor little lad hedn't
shooted an' tell'd him.   Afoor he'd been a
munth wi' us I was as stall'd as a dog o'
seein' him aboot plaace.   It was won body's
wark takkin' care on him, an' at last I says,
" If things isn't different soon, I shall hev'
to keäp a lad to tent him, an' seä him up to
toon an' by agaan, fer ivry mo'tal thing
aboot yard knaws 'at he's frighten'd to deäd
o' owt 'at goäs o' fower legs, an' plaays up

as soon as thaay seäs him a cummin'.''
Well, won daay i' haay-time, when I was at
far end o' th' Black-Sykes agen raailway,
settin' a gang o' wimmin on to the'r wark,
th' lad 'at was drivin' reäper gets off, an'
leäves the hosses by the'rsens wi'oot lowsin'
'em, whilst he goäs fer a drink o' cowd teä.
An' afoor he'd gotten back ageän th' quick
traain fra Sooth cums by, an' hosses hears
it, an' off thaay goäs as hard as thaay can
teär, wi' reäper efter 'em.   My heart to'n'd
cleän ower, fer thaay was mekin' strīght fer
gaate-steäd, an' oor little Jack was set
plaayin' fair i' middle o' th' roäd.   I runn'd
that daay till I o'must bursted mysen, bud
just when I was bet I seäs curate hed gotten
theare, an' nobbud just i' time an' all. He'd
been a walkin' i' gardin, wheare he hedn't
noä neäd to be scarr'd o' nowt, if he kep'
awaay fra beä-skeps, an' he hears hosses

gallopin' like mad and seäs bairn i' front
on 'em, an' oot he runs, wi' niver a thowt o'
his awn daanger, an' flings hissen betwixt
Jack an' hosses an' tries to stop 'em. Bud
he misses clickin' houd o' the'r heads, an'
nobbud maks 'em swarve a bit to won side,
an' reäper, 'at's swingin' ahind 'em, cums wi'
it fingers agen his legs, an' cuts him
o'must i' peäces afoor I knaw'd what he
was up to. Well, we gets him carried i'to
th' hoose, moor deäd then alive, an' ligs
him doon upo' his bed, an' then I gallops
off opo' th' graay fer doctor. An' when
doctor cums he says, " You mun send fer
his muther, an' she mun cum as quick as
iver she can." An' soä I goäs doon to
staation an' telegraphs. An' next daay I
meets ivry traain, an' she cums at noon—
a little bit o' a woman, wi' white hair,
just such 'n anuther as my awn muther.

An' when she seäs me stannin' waaitin',
she begins to shak' like trem'lin'-gress,
an' says, "He's not deäd, is he?" An'
I says, "Doctor says 'at wi' care an'
kindness he'll cum roond yit; an' he'll get
boäth under my roof-tree, mak' yersen
sewer o' that." It was a lee aboot doctor,
though; he hedn't said nowt o' soort.
Nobbud I couldn't stan' there an' tell her
'at her bairn was deein'. Then I lifts her
i'to cart, an' brings her hoäm. An' my
missis taks her to th' lad bed-side. Doon she
goäs o' her knees, an' looks an' looks at him
as if she'd niver ha' dun lookin', an' me
an' my wife slips oot an' leäves 'em aloän
wi' the'rsens.

Bud efter a bit she cums doon stairs,
an' begins to thank us fer what we've dun
fer her bairn, an' tells us what a deäl he'd
reckon'd on us, an' all he'd said i' his letters.

F

An' then my wife fetches little Jack an'
says, " We've nobbud this one left, an' if it
hedn't been fer him as is liggin' up stairs
yonder, he'd ha' been i' che'chyard wi' Tom
an' Annie." An' then they boath on 'em
begins to cry, an' I thinks 'at I'll just seä
what lads is doin', soä oot I goäs an' leäves
'em to it. Well, curate took a to'n efter
his muther cum'd an' begun to mend, an'
her an' my wife no'ssed him up an' fed him
till he could get aboot agaan. He didn't
want fer nowt whilst he was i' oor hoose,
you maay depend. An' when doctor said as
how he mun hev' new milk an' cream an'
things, my wife, 'at's as near as near aboot
owt 'at 'll bring her in a bit o' butter-
munny, niver says nowt, but gies Jack a
kiss an's off to the dairy to th' red coo's
pancheon afoor doctor gets wo'ds oot 'n his
mooth. Soä he eäts an' drinks an' teks

doctor's-stuff till he's o'must well agaan, an'
then off he goäs to seä-side wi' his muther.
But afoor thaay starts I says to him, " I've
gone to chappil all my time, bud noo I'll
tek it to'n an' to'n aboot wi' che'ch. I can
do that fer yĕ, if I can't do nowt else."
An' he laughs, an' then he colours up an'
says, " I nobbud did my duty." Bud I kep'
to what I said, an' me an' my wife teks
Jack to che'ch reg'lar i' a mornin', an' goäs
to chappil at neet. Ey, I've oftens laughed
at parsons, bud I've larnt different noo.

A PEÄCE ABOOT POÄCHIN'.

———<small>•◦•</small>———

TALK o' thy poächin'! Why, mun, if thoo hed been o' No'thside when As'by gang was upo' goä thoo wo'd ha' knawd what real poächin' was. Noo-a-daays if a man gets a hare or two he thinks 'at he's dun sum'ats to swagger on. Bud ther' wasn't noä keäpers i' all cuntry-side as do'st faace that theare lot, nayther by neet nor by daay. An' if by chanche won on 'em was ta'en, why t'uthers clubb'd an' paaid fine; an' if it was a job at liggin' it oot, thaay kep' his wife an' bairns all time he was i' jaail. Ther' was aboot ten on 'em i' all, an' Bob Kendal was best man amung 'em. If ther' was a hare i' toonship, he was sewer to hev'

his ee on her, an' afoor very long she'd
putten her heäd thruf a wire necklaace as
he'd setten i' won o' her runs.   Bob nearly
scarr'd owd Squire Holeigh to deäd, when
him an' his keäper was oot shootin' won
daay.   Thaay seed Bob fire at a hare, an'
goä an' pick her up when she roll'd ower,
soä thaay hides the'rsens an' waaits.   An'
when he cums up hedge-side oot jumps
keäper an' gets houd on him, an' Squire ligs
his awn gun doon, an' teks Bob's an' fires
barril off i' th' air.   Bud when he seäs
what's up, Bob just slips oot 'n his coät, an'
hes houd o' Squire's gun i' a jiffy.   An'
then he tells 'em boäth he'll shoot 'em deäd
if thaay doesn't promise to gie him his
gun agaan, an' let him cleän off an' all.
He look'd that awk'ard 'at thaay seed he
wo'd stick to what he said, an' nayther
Squire nor his man hed pluck o' a moose

i' the'r bellies; soä thaay hed to sweär 'at
thaay'd niver saay nowt aboot this here
little business.   Bud, awiver, when thaay'd
gotten well oot o' gun-shot, thaay begun to
think better on what thaay'd promised.
An' when it cum'd to, thaay hed Bob up at
magistraates' meetin', an' gev oot it was all
his lees when he tell'd foäks how things
was.   We alus know'd which on 'em spok
trewth though; fer ther' was them as was
warkin' at them raailway arches, across
common yonder, 'at hed seed all fraay an'
knoow'd 'at Bob hed raight on it.

I've seen gang oot mysen, wi' nets an'
dogs, times enew; bud it wasn't wo'th my
while to let on to onybody, an' I'd alus a
rabbit fer th' axin, an' soä hed uther foäks
as could keäp a still tung i' the'r heäds.
Things is different noo; bud i' them daays
we hed straange fine sprees, an' we wasn't

noän th' wo's fer it, 'at I can seä. Won time th' As'by lot an' Wraay's gang fra Brigg was oot saame neet, an' got agaate o' fallin' oot, an' keäpers fra Scawby heerd 'em an' cum'd up. Well, when Bob Kendal seäs 'em, he calls oot to Wraay, an' says, " Here's a bigger bill then your's cum'd in to be sattl'd, an' I reckon you'll hev' to help to paay it." Then boäth lots sets to an' leathers keäpers, an' when thaay'd dun wi' them thaay to'ns to agaan an' baastes won-anuther till sum on 'em can hardlins get hoäm. Five or six on 'em was ta'en next daay ; fer yĕ seä thaay was fair to knaw, wi' the'r black ees and bludy heäds : bud when thaay cum'd afoor magistraates next justice daay, Sir Henry an' owd Corfield was ower pleäsed wi' taale to lig owt on very heavy, though i' a gen'ral waay thaay was deäd on poächers.

JACK TO'NER.

—————

DRUNK ageän is he? Well, if he 's boond to kill hissen i' that how, he mud as well do it afoor he's gotten thrif ivry bit o' th' munny his wife browt him. Poor thing, I niver seä her wi'oot thinkin' what a nīst widder she'd mak if owt happen'd to him. An' sum'ats is tied to happen afoor long, if he carries on at this raate.

Not bud what I've heerd foäks saay as God teks care o' little bairns an' drunkards, an' seäs 'em saafe hoäm when thaay hev'n't sense to help the'rsens.

Didn't I niver tell yĕ aboot Jack To'ner as was saaved fra bein' mo'der'd wi' gettin' fresh one Horncastle fair? He'd

been sellin' a string o' hosses—rare good
uns thaay was an' all—an' he'd gotten a
biggish price for 'em. It was war-time, yĕ
knaw, when them French deälers was buyin'
up ivry likely tit 'at thaay could leet on.
Thaay didn't seäm to mind a bit o' a
bump, or a chipp'd knee, an' thaay gev'
Jack o'must all he axed, an' a sight moor
then he'd reckon'd o' gettin'. Well, when
money 's paaid he puts it i'to a sample-
bag, rams it i'to his pocket, an' goäs aboot
pricein' blood-hosses an' gallowaays, till at
last he cums to a eäght-year-owd mare—an'
a real pictur she was—cleän-bred, but wi'
plenty o' boän—an' Jack thinks to hissen,
"Yon's just th' mare fer Squire Killing-
holme." An' he gets talkin' wi' two men
'at's wi' her, and wants to knaw what
thaay 're axin' fer her. An' he tells 'em
it's poonds too much, 'at she was a good

un afoor she was spoilt wi' ower much wark
—onybody could seä that; bud noo she's fit
fer nowt bud to draw a poäny-carri'ge fer
an' owd laady as hes bowt an annuity, an'
hesn't nowt bud her blessin' to leäve to her
relaations.   An' then he hes a look at
t'uther hosses i' fair; bud efter a bit he cums
back an' axes if thaay wean't tek ony less
fer mare.   She's ower owd fer him; he
wants sum'ats 'at's gotten it best years afoor
it, not a brokken-doon thing like yon; bud
still she hes been a good mare i' her time,
an' she isn't a bad un to look at noo; an'
as it isn't fer hissen he wants her, he does
n't mind givin' 'em a goodish price.   Then
thaay stood an' argled a peäce; bud thaay
couldn't cum to noä figure 'at look'd like
bargaining, an' at last thaay goäs i'to
Gouden Cup fer a drink, an' sits doon an'
hes a glass or two.   Awiver, thaay could

n't get price sattled, soä at last Jack says,
" Well, I wean't gie a penny moor then I've
tell'd yĕ, tek it or leäve it. Bud if yĕ can't
mek up yer minds which waay it's to be
noo, yĕ mun stan' fair to-daay, an' I'll stan'
wo'd at my figure till to-morrer. Yĕ knaw
wheare I live, an' I'm saafe to be at hoäm i'
mornin'; nobbud if yĕ'll saay wo'd noo yĕ can
hev' munny doon. It's here i' my pocket."

Well, coupers says thaay'll tek chanche
o' sellin' her i' fair, an' let him knaw afoor
next noon. Then thaay've anuther glass
wi' him, an' goäs back to mare. Bud Jack
gets talkin' wi' Ned fra Ho'den, Dick
Woodhus, an' a lot moor 'at he hesn't seen
sin' last fair-time. An' thaay sits smookin'
an' drinkin', an' braggin' on the'r hosses
an' prices thaay've maade, till sum on 'em
's hed as much as thaay can very well carry,
an' mebbe a drop or two moor.

Jack was alus steady enif i' a gen'ral
waay, bud he was ower fond o' good
cump'ny ; an' he stops listenin' to taales, an'
songs, an' things, till, when it's time to be
gooin', he hesn't right ewse o' his legs, an'
as soon as he gets upo' his feät doon he
cums club-lunch upo' floor an' bashes his
hat in. Well, thaay helps him up, an'
strīghtens oot his hat, an' manages to get
him oot upo' door-step ; bud afoor he's fair
i' streät, doon he cums ageän an' blacks his
ee upo' scraaper. " I can't hev' this," says
landlord. " Whativer shall we do wi'
him ? Plaace is that ram full o' cump'ny
I can't let him be tum'lin aboot i' bar, an'
he 's saafe to get tekken up if he staays
ootside i' th' streät."

Then Woodhus says, " Me an' Tim
Elliot an' Crookleshanks is gooin' doon to
Frank Beän's, an' we mud as well goä roond

by Jack's hoose an' seä him saafe hoäm."
Well, thaay sets Jack upo' his legs ageän,
an' Elliot gets upo' won side an' Crookleshanks upo' t'uther, soä as he can't very
well cum doon, an' off thaay sets. An' at
fo'st thaay got him along pretty fair—he
was daazed like wi' fallin' aboot, an' that
kep' him quiet, an' pleäcemen isn't very
partic'ler at fair-time, yĕ knaw, an' it hed
gotten middlin' dark an' all. Bud when
thaay'd tekken him oot 'n toon thaay'd
bonny wark wi' him, an' noä mistaake.
He'd nowt better to do then to begin
reäpin up owd bygones agen Crookleshanks;
an' then he sets hissen doon by roäd-side,
an' says he isn't a gooin' a step fo'ther till
thaay've hed it oot. Then Crookleshanks
gets mad an' all, an' starts a taale as long
as fra here to Lunnun an' as stallin' as
heavy dumplin's, all aboot Jack an' a mare

an' foäl thaay'd been i' co aboot. An' thaay
went on at wonanuther till Woodhus says
he'll leäve 'em to it if Jack doesn't get up
off 'n bank, an' behaave as he hed owt.
An' then Jack does get up, an' gies
Woodhus, as wasn't expectin' owt o' soort,
a crack upo' th' heäd wi' his fist, an' knocks
him i'to dyke-bottom, an' sets off doon
laane by hissen.

Woodhus an' Crookleshanks was that
mad thaay swoor thaay wo'dn't hev nowt
moor to do wi' him ; bud Elliot, as hedn't
happen'd owt, tell'd 'em 'at thaay mudn't
tak noä noätice on him; an' soä thaay
follows him doon roäd, nobbud thaay keäps
a goodish bit behind him, an' lets him walk
wi' hissen. An' afoor long, Jack teks to
shootin' an' singin', till yer couldn't hear
yersen speäk; but all of a sudden like,
when he gets roond yon to'n wheare owd

willer stump graws, he stops, an' calls oot
sum'ats i' a different waay—thaay niver
knaws what—bud next minute thaay hear
'at he's doon o' grund, an' 'at two or three
foäks is a-top on him robbin' him.

Elliot alus tell'd me he niver knaw'd
what cum next; bud, awiver, he fun' hissen
wi' his hand i' a man's neckhan'kercher, an'
he was a twistin' it till it was that tight he
o'must maade as good a job on it as Mar-
wood maks at Lincoln.

Crookleshanks hed dropp'd on t'uther
chap, an' was giein' him a taaste o' his esh-
plant, and Woodhus was tryin' to get Jack
upo' his feät. Well, when Jack hed cum'd
roond a bit, an' gotten his wind agaän,
Woodhus shuts off across cloäsins to Jack's
hoose, an' gets lads to bring poäny an' cart,
an' a lantern. An' when he gets by agaän
wi' em he teks leet an' houds it doon, an'

looks at men thaay've catch'd. An' if it wasn't them two as hed tried to sell blood-mare to Jack!

Thaay knaw'd he'd gotten his munny i' his pocket, yĕ seïi, an' his hoose was a loän plaace, an' thaay maade sewer o' leetin' on him by hissen afoor he got hoäme. An' he was kickin' up such 'n a shine as he cum'd along 'at thaay niver heerd t'uther men behind him. An' soïi gettin' a drop too much that daay was luckicst thing Jack iver did i' his life. Not bud what drink's straange an' bad i' a gen'ral waay fer them as can't carry it wi'oot lettin' the'r soft cum to top.

TH' OWD WOMAN 'AT COULD CURE TOOTHAACHE.

GOTTEN toothaache agaan, hev yĕ? Well, just do what I tell yĕ, an' you'll be shut o' paain i' a jiffy. It's a reäl good cure, an' I niver knaw'd it faail wi' them as tried it. Owd Fan Jackson, her as liv'd doon by beck, fun' it oot fo'st off, when her husband was that bad wi' paain i' his faace he didn't knaw wheare to put hissen.

Th' owd woman was stall'd past beärin' o' seein' him traffickin' in an' oot, an' up an' doon, ower her cleän floor; soä at last she says to him, "I knaw what'll stop stangin'. Thoo mun hing clock-waaight upo' tooth. That'll null paain if owt will." "I niver

G

heerd tell o' curin' faaceaache that how,"
says owd man. "Didn't tĕ?" says she.
"Why, it's best thing oot by a long waay."
"Well," says owd man, "theare isn't nowt
like tryin'." Then owd woman teks clock-
waaight, an' catgut band it hung by, oot'n
clock, an' hanks it roond tooth—an' a real
greät owd tooth it was an' all, o'must like a
hoss's. "Noo, mind thysen," says she; "I
mun set waaight doon steady upo' taable,
soä as it weant swag." An' she meks as if
she was gooin' to put it doon that eäsy he
wo'dn't niver knaw owt aboot it. Bud
i'steäd o' settin' it upo' taable, she flings it
i'to floor as hard as she can, an' oot flies
tooth i' a crack. Owd man was a bit afoor
he knaw'd if she'd fetch'd his jaw off or noa;
bud, my wo'd, didn't he saay a thing or two
as soon as he could speäk! Awither, toothaache was gone, sure enif.

TOM'S CONVARSION.

I'VE niver been convarted mysen, an' I doän't knaw I'm ony wo's fer that; bud wonce a partic'ler friend o' mine was browt in at chappil, an' it was finest spree him an' me was iver consarn'd in.

It was i' this how it cum aboot. A lot o' foaks hed c'llected munny, an' built the'rsens a chappil; an' ther' wasn't nowt to be said agen that, yĕ knaw. Nobbud when thaay'd gotten it dun thaay begun to think the'rsens a straange sight bigger an' religiouser then uther foäks. An' at last sum on 'em got that owerbeärin' ther' wasn't noä livin' i' saame parish wi' 'em.

Well, Tom says to me won daay, when

we was a knockin' oot beäns wi' flaails i' th'
owd thack barn. "I can't stan' this noä
moor. Here's owd Hard-Fist been knaggin'
at me aboot this here religion agaan. I'll
gie him his fill on it afoor anuther weäk's
oot, just thoo mind if I doïn't." "What
art tĕ up to noo?" says I. "Doïn't get
thysen i'to ony truble. My owd gran'-
muther 'at larnt me th' Loord's Prayer, alus
tell'd me to keäp clear o' gaame-presarves,
magistraates, and chappil-foäks, an' she hed
raight on it too." "Well, mun," says he,
"I'm that stall'd o' theäse here goins'-on 'at
I'm boond to drop on 'em afoor I've dun,
an' if it hes to be, it mud as well be soon as
laate. Then he tells me to mind and be at
cross-tree, hairf a noor afore foäks went i'to
chappil o' Sunda' neet, an' off he goäs wi'
anuther seck o' beäns. That was upo'
Tho'sda'; an' when I was at th' Horn o'

Setterda' neet I heerd as Tom hed gotten religion powerful, an' 'at preächers and ivrybody was that setten up wi' it thaay could hardlin's beär the'rsens.

Well, I niver let on 'at I'd heerd owt aboot it, bud when I gets oot'n hoose I leäns agen wall and laughs fit to split mysen; an' then I goäs to seä Tom, bud he wo'dn't tell me nowt, an' he looked that solid I was o'must fear'd 'at what foäks was sayin' was trew.

Awiver, I cum'd to think diff'rent o' Sunda'. When I gets to cross-tree, theare was Tom an' two or three moor, waaitin' fer me; an' Tom says to us: "I've nobbud gotten this here to saay. When yĕ hear me beginnin' to talk—an' yĕ'll be saafe to do that afoor I've dun—you just houd door to, an' doän't let noäbody oot, not if it's iversoä." Then he seäs owd Hard-Fist

cumin' along toon-streät, an' he begins
tellin' us as how he's left off his wicked
waays an' 's tekken up wi' religion. An'
'at he doesn't think such 'n a sinner as him
can be saaved along wi' reg'lar chappil
foäks, bud 'at he's gooin' to do his best to
get a good plaace i' heaven. An' then him
an' owd Hard-Fist goäs i'to chappil, an'
leäves us wi' wersens ootside.

Well, when all foäks hed gotten i'to
the'r seäts, an' door was shutten to, me an'
my maates went an' stood an' listen'd. An'
at fo'st off things went on reg'lar like, bud
efter sarmon I heerd preächer saay : " Ey,
he's been a greät sinner, bud he'll do
different noo ; " an' then Tom gets up an'
begins to tell his exper'ence. At startin'
he groän'd fit to lift roof off, bud efter a bit
he got warm an' sattl'd doon to his wark,
an' then, my wo'd, didn't he let 'em hear

th' length o' his tung! "It's ivry wo'd on
it trew," says he, "I hev been a bad un,
an' noä mistaake ; bud, Loord, here's dozens
o' foäks i' this chappil 'at calls the'rsens
religious 'at's been as bad as me, an' wo's
an' all, an' Thoo mun excuse me, Loord.
I've lee'd like a good un wheniver I've hed
chanche to mak' owt by it, bud I niver got
six months at Kett'n, like Sep Barker 'at
swore false agen his sister husband. Ey,
Loord, I'm fair grufted in wi' sin, bud I
niver stoäl a flick o' bacon fra a widder
woman, as Kester Watson did when he
robb'd his awn muther." An' then he
groäns agaan wo's than iver, an' foäks begins
to want to get oot 'n chappil. Bud we
houds to door agen 'em, an' he teks a fresh
start, an' belders oot till yĕ could ha' heerd
him fair across toon-streät : "Ey, Loord, I
knaw I've been cloäse wi' my munny, bud I

niver let noä bairn o' mine dee on parish,
lik Sam fra Top Farm ; an' if I hev'n't dun
as I hed owt, I've niver carried on like owd
Natty Hard-Fist, an' him a married man
too. Soä, Loord, if tě can saave th' likes
o' them Thoo mon't forget a deäcent chap
like me." Well, I couldn't houd oot noä
moor. I hed to let the sneck goä, an' sit
doon upo' door-step an' laugh till I was as
weet as muck wi' sweat. An' them as was
i'side was that mad they pull'd door awaay
fra t'uther lads, an' oot thaay cums, won a
top o' anuther. Owd Hard-Fist, an' Kester
Watson, an' that lot, was i' fo'st flight; an'
thaay alus let Tom aloane efter that. An'
fer a good peäce thaay wasn't as setten on
bringin' foäks in as thaay hed been afoor,
nayther.

TH' YALLER-LEGG'D COCK'RIL.

He's a good hand at swaggerin' hissen off, he is. Bud it'll be happenin' to him as it happen'd to th' yaller-legg'd cock'ril, if he doesn't mind what he's aboot.

What soort'n a taale's that, do yĕ saay? Why, it's a peäce 'at my gran'-feyther offens tell'd me when I was a little lad at hoäme.

Yaller-legg'd cock'ril liv'd i' frunt yard wi' owd white cock 'at was his feyther, an' red cock liv'd o' steäm-hoose side o' yard. An' won daay, when owd cock's sittin' crawin' upon crew-yard gaate, cock'ril gets up an' begins to craw an' all. "Cock-a-doodle-do," says owd cock. "Kick-a-ee-a-ee," says cock'ril; he couldn't craw plaain

yit, he was ower yung. " Houd thy noise,"
says owd cock, as couldn't abeär to hear
him skreelin' like yon. " Houd thy noise.
Bairns should be seän an' not heerd." Soä
cock'ril, 'at thinks as he's doin' on it fo'st
raate, hes to get off gaate an' tek up wi' th'
hens an' chickens agaan. An' owd cock
craws and craws, till at last cock fra t'uther
side o' yard cums to knaw what's up. Bud
when he seäs who it is 'at's makkin' all to-
do, he reckon's 'at he's nobbud dropp'd in
by chanche, an' passes time o' daay; an'
then says as how he mun goä and seä if
garthman isn't sarvin' pigs, an' if he hesn't
slatter'd a few taaties an' things 'at 'll mak
a dinner fer that theare last cletch 'at graay
hen's browt off. An' soä he teks his hook
back agaain to steäm-hoose yard.

Bud daay efter, when owd cock's gone a
peäce o' waay doon sandy laane wi' a pullet

'at's lookin' fer a nest, cock'ril flies upo'
gaate agaan, an' claps his wings an' craws
till th' hens is o'must stoäne-deäf. Fo'st
won on 'em tell'd him to cum doon an'
then anuther, bud it wasn't noä good: he
was that setten upo' hearin' hissen 'at he
niver hed noä time to listen to onybody else.
Awiver, just when he reckon'd 'at he'd
gotten to do it o'must as well as his feyther,
or mebbe a bit better, up cums cock fra
t'uther side o' yard wi' all his neck-feathers
up, an' he says to cock'ril, "I thowt I
heerd yĕ at it yesterdaay, an' noo I knaw I
did; cum on." An' afoor cock'ril could
get oot anuther craw, red cock hed him off
gaate an' doon i' crew-yard. An' when
he'd gotten him theare, he wasn't long afoor
he'd maade an' end o' him. An' when owd
cock cum'd hoäm he fun' pigs just finishin'
cock'ril's yaller legs, an' he heerd red cock

crawin' like mad upo' steäm-hoose wall.
"A-deary-me," says he, "I knaw'd how it
would be if he wouldn't keäp his tung still.
Well, you uther chickens mun tak warnin'
by him, an' mind what I tell yĕ: Niver craw
till yer spurs is grawn."

OWD-FASHION'D RIDDLES FOR OWD-FASHION'D FOÄKS.

———•~—

Question: As I was gooin' ower Lunnun
       Brig,
    I met a loäd o' sou'jers:
    Sum i' ickits, sum i' ackits,
    Sum i' red an' yaller jackits—
       What was thaay?
Answer: Why, a swarm o' wasps.

Question: As I was gooin' ower Lunnun
       Brig,
    I look'd in at a winder,
    An' fower an' twenty laadies
    Was dancin' on a cinder—
       What was thaay?
Answer: Sparks i' fire-graate.

Question: She's black an' breet,
An' runs wi'oot feet—
What's that?

Answer: A flat-iron.

Question: Roond th' hoose,
An' roond th' hoose,
An' i' cupboard?

Answer: Why, it's a moose.

Question: Fower an' twenty white beäs'
Stannin' i' a stall,
Fower an' twenty white beäs'
An' red un licks 'em all?

Answer: Th' teäth an' th' tung.

Question: As black as ink, an' isn't ink ;
As white as milk, an' isn't milk ;
As soft as silk, an' isn't silk ;
An' hops aboot like a filly foal—
What's yon?

Answer: A magpie.

Question: Black I am, and much admired;
    Men do seek me till thaay're
      tired;
    Tire horse, an' tire man;
    Lowse me riddle if tĕ can.
Answer: Coäl.

Question: Roond th' hoose,
    An' roond th' hoose,
    And in at parlour winder—
      What's that?
Answer: Why, sunshine, to be sewer.

Question: Creäp thrif hedge an' steäl corn,
    Little coo wi' leather horns—
      What's you?
Answer: A hare.

Question: Under watter, ower watter,
    An' niver tuches watter—
      What's that?

Answer: Why, a lass gooin' ower a brig
wi' a paail o' watter o' her
heäd.

Question: Red wi'in, an' red wi'oot,
Fower corners roond aboot?
Answer: Why, that's a brick.

Question: As I was gooin' ower Lunnun
Brig,
I sees a little red thing;
I picks it up, an' sucks it blud,
An' leäves it skin to dry.—
What's yon?
Answer: That's an oringe.

Question: As I was gooin' ower Westminster Brig,
I chanch'd o' a Westminster
scholar;

He pull'd off his hat, *an' drew* off
    his glove,
An' wish'd me good-morrer.
Tell me his naame, fer I've
    tell'd it to you.

Answer: His name was Andrew.

Question: I heerd a greät rumle,
    As I was gooin' ower Hum'er
    Three pots a boilin'
    An' noä fire under—
        What was that?

Answer: Watter under boät.

Question: When I was gooin' thrif a cloäse
        o' wheät,
    I pick'd up sum'ats 'at's good to eät,
    It wasn't fish, flesh, bo'd, nor boän;
    I kep' it till it run aloän?

Answer: Yon mun ha' been a egg.

II

Question: As I went thrif oor gardin gap,
            I met my Uncle Ned,
            Wi' pins an' neädles up'n his back,
            An' he kep' joggin' a-head?
Answer: That was a pricky-otchin.

Question: Roond th' hoose,
            An' roond th' hoose,
            An' leäves a white gluv i' winder?
Answer: That's snaw.

Question: Roond th' hoose,
            An' roond th' hoose,
            An' leäves a black gluv i' winder?
Answer: That's raain.

Question: Black wi'in, an' red wi'oot,
            Fower corners roond aboot—
            What's yon?
Answer: Th' chimley.

Question: Black wi'in, an' black wi'oot,
Fower corners roond aboot,
An' a white spot i' middle—
What's that?

Answer: Uven wi' a caake i' it.

Question: Black wi'in, an' black wi'oot,
Three legs an' a iron cap?

Answer: A black pot.

Question: Full o' hoïles, an' houds watter—
What's that?

Answer: Recken-hook. It houds all watter 'at's i' pot ower fire.

Question: A riddle, a riddle, as I suppoäse,
Fifty ees an' niver a noïse?

Answer: That's a wire sieve.

Question: Tho'ty white hosses upon a red hill,
        Noo thaay goä, noo thaay goä,
        noo they stan' still?
Answer: Them's yer teäth.

Question: Ten men's length, an' ten men's
        strength,
        An' ten men can't rear it?
Answer: A waggon roäpe.

Question: Brass cap, an' wooden head,
        Spits fire, an' spews lead?
Answer: A gun.

Question: Graws i' wood, whinnies i' th'
        moor,
        An' goäs up an' doon oor hoose
        floor—
        What's that?
Answer: A sweepin'-brush maade on hosshair.

Question : Graws i' wood, an' yowls i'
            toon,
        An' addles it maister many a
            croon ?

Answer : A fiddle wi' cat-gut strings.

Question : My ribs is lin'd wi' leather,
        I've a hoïle i' my side,
        An' I'm offens wanted—
           What's my naame ?

Answer : A pair o' bellers.

Question : Mother, feyther, sister, brother,
        All runnin' efter wonanuther,
        An' can't catch wonanuther ?

Answer : Mill-saayles.

Question : As I went oot, soä I cum'd in,
        An' oot'n th' deäd I seed th'
           livin' spring ;

Seven ther' was, an' six ther' be,

Tell me riddle, an' then hang me.

Answer : A bo'd 'at's maade it nest i' a deäd
hoss, an's gotten five yung
uns.

Question : Riddle me, riddle me ree,

Tell me what my riddle's to
be—-

It'll goä thruf a rock, thruf a
reel,

Thruf an owd woman's spinnin'-
wheel,

Thruf a milner's hopper,

Thruf a bag o' pepper,

Thruf an owd mare's shink-shank
boän ;

Such a riddle hev I knawn.

Answer : A worm. Worm's 'll get thruf
owt.

Question : It is i' th' oyster, bud not i' th'
shell ;

It is i' the clapper, bud not i' th'
bell ;

It is i' th' church, bud not i' th'
steäple ;

It is i' th' parson, bud not i' th'
peöple ;

It is i' th' rock, bud not i' th'
stoäne ;

It is i' th' marrow, bud not i' th'
boäne ;

It is i' th' bolster, bud not i' th' bed;

It isn't in livin', nor yit i' th' deäd.

Answer : The letter R.

Question : Itum Parditum all cloäth'd i'
green,

Th' King couldn't reäd it, nor
madam, th' Queen ;

Thaay sent fer wise men oot'n th' Eäst,
'At said it hed horns, bud it wasn't
a beäst—
What's that?
Answer : Why, prick-holly.

Question : When's a uven not a uven?
Answer : When she's agaate.

Question : Which side on a sheäp does most
wool grow on?
Answer : Why, ootside to be sewer, bairn.

Question : As I was gooin' ower Borring-
ham Ferry,
I heerd a thing saay "Chit-a-ma-
cherry;"
Wi' doony han's, an' doony faace,
A white cockade, an' silver laace?
Answer : A monkey.

Question : What's that as is black, an'
white, an' red all over ?

Answer : A newspaaper. It's white paaper,
black ink, an' when you've
dun readin' it, it's read all
over.

A LINCOLNSHEER LETTER.

———•◦•———

Dick, thoo's o'must forgotten th'owd plaace,
    I'm thinkin', noo.
Dost mind 'at we plaay'd i' th' crewyard,
    an' rid o' th' red poll-coo,
Wi' a bit o' band fer a bridle ? An', Dick,
    dost tĕ mind thoo was scarr'd
When I call'd up th' pigs to eät thĕ, if iver
    we went thrif yard ?

Dost mind 'at we went to catch bull-heäds
    wi' a tar-marl line, an' a preg
Thoo stoäl fra oot 'n th' oät-stack, an' th'
    nettles tang'd thy leg,
An' I tell'd thĕ it was a judgment fer
    steälin' yon preg fer me ?—

I'm thinkin', Dick, 'at ofens I was straange
    an' hard o' thee.

Dost mind owd Drummer, an' Blackbo'd,
    an' white-faced foäl, an' mare
'At feyther bowt o' th' Squire an' sell'd at
    th' 'tAndra Fair ?
Well, things is straange an' chaanged, Dick :
    Miss Kaate an' th' Squire's deäd,
An' yung Squire's gotten greät lads o' hes awn,
    an' he's gettin' graay hairs i' his heäd.

An' parson, he's dun up th' che'ch, Dick,
    till it's o' must as good as new ;
An' putten in fresh oäk seäts, Dick, i' stead
    o' yon owd broon pew,
Wheare we crack'd wer nuts i' door-sneck,
    and plaay'd marbils, an' read yon taale,
O' th' she-beär swallerin' all them bairns,
    an' Joänah 'at liv'd i' a whaale.

Th' esh-tree 'at grew i' th' hoss-cloase blew
    up i' th' wind last fall,
An' Polly—thoo hesn't forgotten—she's
    wedded an' widder'd an' all :
Foäks ses she'd ha' dun a deäl better, to
    tak thee i'steäd o' her Jim ;
Bud all's fer th' best, an' she's gotten good
    riddance an' shuttance o' him.

It's tho'ty year sin' thoo went, Dick, cum
    next owd Lammas-daay—
Tho'ty year sin' thoo'd wo'ds wi' her, an'
    took off to Americaay—
An' mebbe if thoo cum'd back, Dick, to seä
    th' owd toon an' plaace,
I shouldn't knaw it was thoo, Dick, an'
    shouldn't remember thy faace.

An' 'Mericaay's hunderds an' hunderds o'
    miles awaay ower seä fra here,

An' mebbe I shouldn't fīn' thĕ, Dick, if I
    went to seek thĕ theare.
Thoo'll ha' gotten new waays an' speäks,
    Dick, 'at I shouldn't understand,—
Bud if 'Mericaay is far awaay ther's a
    Kingdom nigh at hand.

We mun mind an' get up theare, Dick, we
    mun mind an' get up theare,
An' then thoo'll tell me all, Dick, thoo's
    dun i' tho'ty year,—
We'll just be bairns together, Dick, together
    thoo an' me;—
When I think o' seäin' thĕ, why, Dick, I'm
    o'must wantin' to dee!

TH' LINCOLNSHEER POÄCHER.

(1881.)

———◆———

" Th' doctors hev' given me ower;
  Thaay tell me I mun dee
  I' th' fower stoane walls o' a prison,
  Wheare ther's nowt—not a floower nor
    a tree;
  I' th' fower stoane walls o' a prison
  Wheare a daaisy 'll niver blaw,
  An' nobbud gress i' th' flag-stoanes
  An' bits o' moss 'll graw.

I'm not afeard o' deein',
  Bud I want to hear agaan
  Th' wind i' th' tops o' th' fir-trees,
  An' smell th' smell o' th' raan

Wheare it cums doon streight fra
    heaven;
I want to hear th' call
O' th' pywipes i' th' marsh-land
An' th' craws ahind th' ploo.
Bud thaay say them daays is ower
An' dun', fer good an' all;
I've nowt bud liggin' here waatin'
An deein' left to do.

Th' parson, he's been to seä me
Wi' a straange queer taale to tell,
O' a narrer rough roäd to heaven
An' a stright, smoothe waay to hell;
Bud, I think, if th' Loord was sarten
'At He wanted us up abuv
He'd keap His roäds a bit better—
An' how can God be luv'
If He maade the devil, an' all them things
'At's creapin' an' crowlin' beloä,

Wheare, parson says, 'at unchristen'd
bairns
An' mo'derers, an' such-like goä?

I'm not agooin' to beleave it
O' Him 'at maade ivrything,
An' set th' sun to shine i' th' sky
An' larnt th' bo'ds to sing ;
Bud I'd rayther be doon wheare th' fire
An' brimstun foriver bo'ns,
An' just goä roond wi' a bucket
An' give foaks drinks by to'ns—
Then sit i' yon stright-maade heaven,
Wheare saints an' aangels sing,
An' niver hear a pheasant craw,
Nor th' skirr o' a partridge wing;
Wheare ther' isn't a bank nor a plantin'-
side
Wheare rabbits cum oot an' plaay,
An' stamp wi' the'r feet o' a moonleet neet.

Wheare it's warm o' th' coudest daay ;
An' th' otchins ligs hid i' winter—
Ther's nowt like this, I doot—
Why, them 'at gets sent up to heaven
Mun be stall'd when a week's runn'd oot.

It's a weary while I've been liggin'
Wi' my faace to a prison wall,
Bud I knaw ootside th' blackheäds cry,
An' it's Spring, an' th' cuckoos call ;—
I' not afeard o' deein'
Bud I straangely want to see
Th' sun cum up ower Ranthrup
Agaan afoor I dee."

PEATER.

You'll gie me twenty poond fer th' bull,
    an' then you'll be buyin' him dear?—
Why, I wo'dn't sell our Peater fer hundreds
    o' poonds a year.

It was Peater 'at saav'd my little lass—my
    little Polly 'at's deäd;
An' Peater 'll fin' his meät i' my crib till
    sods is ower my heäd.

Me an' my wife was at chappil, an' Polly at
    hoäm i' her bed,
An' preächer—I disremember a sight o' th'
    things he said;

Bud he tell'd us o' God an' His goodness,
    His luv an' His wunderful waays,
An' said 'at He help'd th' faaithful noo, as
    He help'd 'em i' Bible-daays.

Th' chappil was swelterin' hot that neet, an'
    I think I was o'must asleäp ;
I thowt I was doon i' th' cloasins, wi' feyther
    a weshin' th' sheäp,

An' feyther's been deäd nigh fifteen year—
    bud I cum'd slap oot'n my dreäm,
Th' bairns thaay begun to belder like owt,
    an' the wimmin begun to screäm.

When sum'ats cum'd teärin' along th' streät,
    an' bolt at th' chappil door,
An' Peater cums bang thrif door-steäd, an'
    doon o' th' chappil floor.

I 2

"It's a message fra God," says preächer,
    "we knaw He gev wo'ds to an ass.
Ey, greät is th' Loord i' His goodness, and
    brings mighty things to pass."

But I ups an' I says to Peater, as mad as I
    iver could be,
"It's likely He'd send a message by a cross-
    bred brewte like thee."

An' I clamm'd fast houd o' th' ring i' his
    noäse, an' started to lug him oot,
An' then, when I'd gotten him up to th'
    door, I seed what he'd cum'd aboot:

Th' sky was a bright as a fo'nis at neet, wi'
    yaller, and po'ple, an' red,
My hoose an' th' staables was all i' a low,—
    an' Polly at hoäm i' her bed!

Me ?—ey, I laamed my back that neet wi'
  fetchin' my Polly doon :
Thaay saay I was blĩnded an' daaz'd by th'
  smook, an' mebbe I jump'd ower soon.

Th' stairs an' th' landin' was all bo'nt awaay
  —well, I was her feyther, you see,
An' I couldn't leäve my Polly up theare i'
  th' fire to dee.

Bud she was nowt to Peater, an' Peater
  saav'd her life
Wi' fetchin' us oot o' th' chappil, an' he'll
  bide wi' me an' my wife,

An' eät his fill i' th' crew-yard, till Peater
  or us is deäd ;
An' soä, if you want him, why then you mun
  waait till th' sods is ower my heäd.

A LAST WO'D.

I KNAW 'at it's written i' God's awn book
    at bastard stocks shall dee,
  But still th' lass is blud o' my blud, an'
    her bairn is boane o' my boane.
I niver hev said 'at she'd dun as she'd owt;
    bud it's not fer th' like o' me,
  To fling to th' door on my gell i' her
    shaame, an' leave her to bear it aloane.

"Th' waages o' sin!"- aw yis, I knaw;
    thaay'll last till her hair is graay;—
  Th' waage 'at she's arn'd, it 'll last till
    she's deïd, an' th' coffin's naail'd to o'
    her faace.

I can't t'on her oot wi' her bairn i' her
  airms, an' co'ss her, an' drive her
  awaay,
   An' Him 'at was good to th' theäf o' th'
     cross, wo'd ha' tell'd yĕ th' saame i'
     my plaace.

" You wean't ha' noä bastards bred up o' yer
  land,—I've gotten enif to do
   Wi' keapin' things gooin', an' addlin' th'
     rent, wi'oot tekkin' luve-bairns in "—
If you hed a doughter i' trubble like her,
  wi' noane i' th' wo'ld bud you
   To look to, you'd fling her oot i'to th'
     streat, an' leäve her to dee i' her sin?

It's likely you wo'd ! bud rich foaks' hearts
  isn't maade like uther men's—
   You gie up yer baabies to sarvants to
     keep, an' mebbe you wo'dn't mind,

An' wo'dn't lig wakken 'at neet i' yer beds,
 an' werrit an' witter yersens,
As long as you'd plenty o' vittles an' cloase,
 'at yer childer was ragged an' pined.

" I mun leäve my land, or th' lass mun
 leäve,—you'll houd by what you've
 said ;
  You wean't put up wi' th' likes o' her,
  —you reckon you're mester here."
Then the land mun goä, an' I'll stan' by
 her,—if her sins is as red as red,
  The Loord, He can wesh 'em as white
  as wool, an' I wean't gie her up—so
  theare !

www.ingramcontent.com/pod-product-compliance
Lightning Source LLC
Chambersburg PA
CBHW030610270326
41927CB00007B/1109